WHAT'S IT LIKE TO BE A

BABY CHIMP?

First published in the UK in 1998 by

 Belitha Press Limited,
London House, Great Eastern Wharf,
Parkgate Road, London SW11 4NQ.

Copyright © in this format
Belitha Press Limited 1998

Editor Honor Head
Designer Hayley Cove
Illustrator Matthew Nicholas
Production Paul Harding
Consultants Sally Morgan and Wendy Body

ISBN 1 85561 763 3

British Library Cataloguing in Publication
Data for this book is available from the
British Library

Printed in Belgium

Photo credits J.J.Alcalay/Bios/Still Pictures: 16.
Gerry Ellis/BBC Natural History Unit: 11, 20.
Thomas Ennis/Getty Images: 7.
Ferrero-Labat/Ardea: 28b.
Jackie Le Fevre/Survival Anglia/OSF: 10.
Michel Gunther/Bios/Still Pictures: 12, 23.
Martha Holmes/BBC Natural History Unit: 15r.
Gerard Lacz/NHPA: 9.
Renee Lynn/Getty Images: 22.
Tom McHugh/Photo Researcher Inc./OSF: 17, 24.
Mark Newman/FLPA: front cover.
K. Owen/Woodfall Wild Images: 4, 28t.
Steve Robinson/NHPA: 21.
Manjoh Shah/Getty Images: 18, 19.
Richard Smithers/Survival Anglia/OSF: 5.
Stockmarket/Zefa: 13, 31.
Adrian Warren/Ardea: 26, 27.
Terry Whittaker/FLPA: 15l.

The illustrator would like to thank
Twycross Zoo, Whipsnade Zoo and
Kew Gardens for their help and advice.

WHAT'S IT LIKE TO BE A
BABY CHIMP?

by Honor Head

Illustrated by
Matthew Nicholas

Belitha Press

Chimpanzees are not monkeys, but a type of ape. Apes don't have tails and their arms are longer than their legs. They live in Africa.

Like human babies, baby chimpanzees have much to learn as they grow up. They also have a lot of fun, playing games and getting up to mischief.

Chimpanzees live in large, caring family groups. This book will help you to understand what it's like to be a chimp and how they live.

When you read this book, imagine that you are a baby chimp. You live in a green, leafy place with lots of trees. It is hot...

When you are born you are
very small and you don't have
much hair. You have a pink
face which will turn black
as you grow older.

The adult chimpanzees make
a great fuss of you. They all
help to look after you and
enjoy playing with you.

When you grow up your body will be covered in long, thick black hair, except for your face, hands and feet.

When you are very small you go everywhere with your mother. You cling to your mother's tummy all the time, even when she swings through the trees.

When you are about five months old, you learn to ride on your mother's back.

As you grow bigger you sometimes slip off and have to climb back on again.

You spend about seven
hours a day eating.
You eat mainly fruit,
seeds and leaves.

You also like a tasty snack of ants. Termites are like big ants and they are one of your favourite foods.

When you find a termite nest, you poke a stick into it. The termites cling to the stick and you lick them off.

When you feel thirsty, the whole family goes to the nearest stream or river.

You drink by sucking up the water through your mouth. You make lots of slurping noises.

As you grow older you learn to use a leaf to scoop up water which is hard to reach.

You also use leaves like a sponge. You chew them until they are soft, then you soak them in water. You use the soft, wet leaves to wash yourself, or to clean a cut that is bleeding.

By the time you are one year old you can walk and climb trees. You usually walk on your hands and feet.

When you walk on all fours, you bend your fingers and walk on your knuckles. You can also walk upright.

You live on the ground
and in the trees.
You learn to swing
from branch to branch
with your long arms.

You have big hands and
feet. Your palms and
the soles of your feet
are pink and hairless.

You have five long
fingers on each
hand and five long
toes on each foot.

Your fingers and toes are long and strong so that you can grip branches and trunks as you swing through the trees.

When it rains you don't run for shelter. Your mother sits with her head down and holds you close to her. You stay snug and dry while she gets soaking wet.

You make all sorts of
noises and pull different
faces to show other
chimps how you feel.

When you want
to play you open
your mouth wide
and laugh.

When you feel scared
or angry you pull back
your lips and show your
teeth. When you find
food to eat you bark
to tell the others.

When you are excited
you shriek and scream.
You bang on trees and
slap the ground.

You have very good eyesight. Your eyes are on the front of your head not on the sides.

This is so that you can see where you are going when you swing through the trees.

You have a very short nose. You use your sense of smell to find fruit trees.

21

You live in a large group of chimp families. Everyone is very friendly and you give each other lots of hugs.

If you want something, you hold out your hand to ask for it.

You say hello in many different ways. Sometimes you touch fingertips when you meet someone.

Sometimes you like to kiss your friends and family and pat them on the back.

You are very playful.
When you are young
your mother plays with
you nearly all day.

Playing helps you
to learn how to do
different things and
to look after yourself.

As you grow older you begin to play with the other baby chimps. You learn to pretend fight.

The adults watch over you as you play and make sure you don't come to any harm.

You love to be groomed. Other chimps look through your hair for bits of twigs or leaves that may be caught there. Sometimes they find a small, itchy insect such as a flea.

You like to have a rest at midday when it is very hot. The family rests together.

At night your mother builds a nest high in the trees for you to sleep in. You have to be careful not to fall out during the night!

The nest is made
of leaves and twigs.
The branches are bent
over to make a bed.

It only takes ten minutes
to make the nest. Your
mother makes a new
one every night.

If you are a girl chimp, you will spend hours helping your mother and learning to do what she does by copying her.

You will have your first baby when you are about 12 years old. You will have a baby about every five years.

Both boys and girls stay with the family group. You all help to look after each other.

You will live for about 40 years and have many children and grandchildren.

INDEX OF USEFUL WORDS

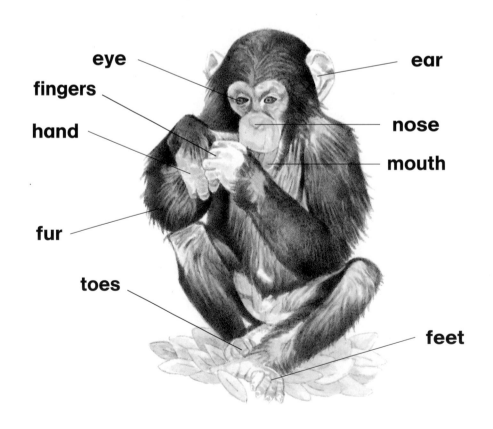

eye

fingers

hand

fur

toes

ear

nose

mouth

feet